How To Manage Money

A Financial Management Program Aimed At Empowering
Young Individuals To Cultivate And Safeguard
Their Economic Resources

(Cease Impulsive Expenditures, Expedite Debt Repayment)

Antoine Robert

TABLE OF CONTENT

You Are Interested In Initiating A Business Venture. 1

What Are Your Genuine Aspirations In Life?............10

Increase The Accumulation Of Assets While Minimizing Liabilities..17

Exemplary Strategies That Illuminate The Path To Wealth 25

How To Effectively Manage Your Finances? An Overview 35

How To Save? 30 Easy Tricks 48

Strategies For Disregarding Advertisements............66

Strategies For Overcoming Impulsive Shopping Patterns..73

What Are The Reasons For The Crucial Significance Of Financial Intelligence?...119

Understanding Credit..135

You Are Interested In Initiating A Business Venture.

Do you possess the concept and the requisite drive, yet what level of financial resources are you intending to allocate towards the development of your startup?

According to a study, a decade ago, the average cost of initiating a small business amounted to $31,150. While it is true that some organizations rely heavily on financial resources to achieve progress, at Inc., we frequently receive testimonials from the founders of rapidly expanding companies who commenced their ventures with a few hundred dollars rather than several thousand.

According to Bert Jacobs, one of the cofounders of Life Is Good apparel company, in the present day, an astute entrepreneur who possesses a website can generate within six months what took us six years to achieve.

The rapid advancement of technology is reducing a significant number of startup expenses, as pointed out by Jacobs. He and his brother John initiated the foundational focus of their enterprise in 1989, with a sum of $200 secured from their sibling, Allan. The past was undeniably challenging, as Jacobs expressed to Inc's Leigh Buchanan.

If we had possessed that technology, we would have employed it. However, we dedicated several years to establishing a company by recruiting individuals we encountered during pickup basketball matches, engaging in lighthearted conversations with potential customers on the streets while remaining vigilant for law enforcement, and seeking guidance from retailers spanning the entire East Coast whom we made impromptu visits to. It arguably lacked efficiency. Undoubtedly, it was not the most efficient. However, many of our company's principles originated from the initial imperative to accomplish tasks inexpensively and through face-to-face interactions.

Life Is Good consistently generates $100 million in clothing sales at present. Furthermore there

especially the roughness and

Some of the perspectives provided by Jacobs include,

tolerance, which remains relevant in contemporary times. If you aspire to commence a business that can eventually rival his success, there is no absolute requirement to expend funds through identical means.

Entrepreneurs who have recently established their organizations concur that contemporary technology is truly exceptional.

In 2016, Matthew Schwab, co-founder and CEO of San Francisco flower delivery startup BloomThat, expressed that it has become significantly easier to embark on entrepreneurial ventures.

Schwab established his organization by leveraging the Stripe payment processing platform, which facilitates the initiation of e-commerce operations for numerous online businesses aimed at marketing goods and services. Furthermore, Stripe is merely one component of the vast ecosystem of technological advantages that serve to facilitate the cost-effective and expedient initiation of your startup; a concept we, at Inc., firmly uphold. Refer to the "moment startup kit": "Designate the "moment startup kit":

Websites, commerce transactions, financial processing, cloud computing, communications, and funding have all been streamlined by platforms such as Squarespace, Slack, Kickstarter,

Dropbox, Amazon's comprehensive Web services division, and PayPal....

Over the past decade, these foundational elements have markedly reduced the time and financial investment required to establish a business, particularly those of an innovative nature. Due to factors such as the emergence of the internet, open-source programming, distributed computing, and evolving trends, several experts calculate that technological initiatives which previously required an investment of $5 million a decade ago can now be accomplished for less than $50,000, as stated in a research paper published by the National Bureau of Economic Research in 2014.

Positive news: It is highly likely that you do not necessitate $5 million in order to commence your business. It is probable that you will not need $50,000 or $30,000 either. To be frank, it is highly likely that only a fraction of that amount will be necessary. According to the statistics from 2014, a mere 49 percent of Inc." According to our annual CEO survey, 500 respondents reported that they allocated less than $5,000 towards launching their businesses. The subsequent largest group, comprising 15% of respondents, indicated their need for a monetary sum ranging from $10,000 to

$50,000.

The amount of cash you desire will vary based on your responses to the following inquiries:

• What type of enterprise are you interested in establishing? • What kind of commercial venture do you aspire to launch? • In what field of commerce do you envision beginning your own business?

• How many individuals do you have to operate your startup? • What is the count of individuals responsible for running your startup? • May I inquire about the total of individuals involved in managing your startup? • Please provide information on the quantity of individuals overseeing operations in your startup.

• May I inquire as to the location of your intended business establishment and the amount of space you require?

• What is the required speed at which you need to bring your product or service to the market?

• What is the maximum duration you can tolerate

live without remuneration? Shall we proceed by addressing each of these inquiries?

What Are Your Genuine Aspirations In Life?

You are not alone in your uncertainty regarding your true aspirations for life. On a daily basis, a substantial number of individuals, potentially reaching into the millions, wander without purpose across the globe. The below recommendations will aid you in discerning your life's objectives, should you wish to avoid aimless wandering throughout your journey.

Be egocentric.

If one consistently sacrifices one's time and ambitions for the sake of others, it can pose a challenge to determine one's true desires and aspirations. It is imperative that you give priority to your needs. If you were not bound by the responsibilities associated with your employment, familial duties, social commitments, or any other obligations, what activities would you currently be engaged in? It is important to remember that it is permissible to prioritize oneself, as it is unlikely that others will do so unless one takes the initiative.

Never look back.

Do not experience any sense of culpability for your self-centeredness. You lead a life. This presents an opportune moment for you to embrace the life you envision and pursue it without constraint. One's inability to progress will persist if they persistently dwell on previous choices or omissions. Refrain from fixating on previous occurrences. Reside in the present moment while also considering the future!

Determine what you require.

Reflect upon your utmost requirements as you take a seat. Is it your household? the capacity to articulate one's thoughts and opinions without constraint? Love? assurance of resources? Another thing?

At times, discerning one's needs can pose a considerable challenge. Hence, this Life Assessment can undeniably provide assistance. By participating in this complimentary assessment, you will acquire the capacity to identify the aspects of your life that necessitate further consideration, as well as the obstacles impeding your pursuit of the desired lifestyle.

Subsequently, you may proceed to generate a roster of prioritized items. In addition, kindly contemplate the nature of the lasting impression you desire to leave in your wake.

Determine the source of your irritation.

By actively opposing something that is contrary to your aspirations, you can elevate yourself to great heights. Identify the sources of your irritation and articulate them clearly. Kindly refrain from simply expressing your strong disdain towards office work. Please provide a detailed explanation for your discontentment. It is possible that your employer's excessive attention to detail and control could be responsible for the issue at hand. Your load of work? Your pointless position title? Alternatively, could all of the aforementioned options be applicable? What are your sources of irritation and what potential resolutions could be implemented? What degree of fixation are you seeking?

Uncover the authentic origins of your happiness.

If one is satisfied with their existence, it signifies the absence of any squandered moments. Your aspirations derive from the extent of your contentment. Take a moment to reflect upon the factors that bring you joy. Does it move? being near young people? having a prosperous business? Your romantic partner? financial flexibility?

Once you pinpoint the one thing that brings you the utmost joy, you will gain precise insight into the ambitions you should pursue in life.

Ensure that those in your vicinity are cognizant of your objectives.

Articulate your ambitions and aspirations to others. Express your thoughts openly! By articulating your objectives to others, you enhance the likelihood of receiving their backing and benefiting from their novel insights. Mother is sometimes right!

Increase The Accumulation Of Assets While Minimizing Liabilities.

Contrary to prevailing public opinion, I contend that an asset can be categorized as a source of income, whereas a liability can be defined as something that incurs an outflow of funds. To put it succinctly, a liability can be likened to a voracious caterpillar that perpetually consumes your finances. That is precisely why a myriad of them is bound to exert substantial strain on your financial resources throughout your lifetime.

In accordance with the aforementioned claim, it is permissible for me to state that a hostel leased to students can be considered an advantageous asset, whereas a residential building would be deemed a financial burden. The distinction between the two can be delineated as follows: In the context of hostel accommodation, students remunerate the landlord for the utilization of amenities, such as paying house rent. Conversely, the landlord compensates the various tradespeople involved in the upkeep of the residential building, including carpenters, upholsterers, electricians, builders, welders, and plumbers, without receiving any form of monetary compensation. This implies that the hostel establishment, along with its associated amenities, operates with the purpose of generating profits for its proprietor, whereas a residential building and its facilities do not prioritize financial gains.

Legend has it that there existed an account chronicling the acquisition of a grand estate valued at $86,000 within an urban metropolis. His acquaintance procured a premises within the identical urban setting, with comparable financial outlay, albeit employing personal resources, to initiate a financial institution. In advanced years, it was documented that the individual who acquired the grand estate experienced financial decline due to the ceaseless requirements for maintaining the property, while his acquaintance prospered exponentially. That is merely scratching the surface when it comes to unraveling the demarcation between an asset and a liability.

Once more, consider the comparison between a commercial bus and a privately owned automobile. The commercial bus is a valuable resource as its primary purpose is to generate a consistent income for its owner, in contrast to the private car owner who expends considerable time and effort on various repairs and upkeep. Similarly, a laptop utilized for the purpose of viewing movies can be considered a burden, as it incurs maintenance expenses that need to be covered. The identical laptop can serve as a valuable resource when utilized for online enterprises or even graphic design purposes. With the provision of these illustrations, I am confident that you will be able to discern additional assets and liabilities independently, thereby enhancing your targeting capabilities.

Nevertheless, one cannot do away with obligations; they are crucial for existence. What you should do is to have them in lesser numbers and, thus, reduce their counterproductive effects. Subsequently, encompass yourself with the abundant resources available globally. Acquire parcels of land at various locations. Buy whole buildings. Buy cargo ships. Participate as a stakeholder in a prominent football club. Build a petrochemical company. The list seems endless.

Chapter 4: Strategies for managing undesired belongings

U

Unwanted property pertains to possessions that are no longer utilized or favored, potentially due to their obsolescence. The list may encompass items such as your compact refrigerator, furniture pieces, garments, footwear, laundry appliance, plastic materials, metal containers, or any similar articles. Kindly refrain from disposing any of them promptly. If you decide to proceed, you will have essentially squandered a portion of your funds.

Should the property in question be non-operational, arrange for the services of a skilled tradesperson to restore and prepare it to a marketable state. Subsequently, transfer ownership by selling it to a third party. That approach effectively allows for the reinvestment of your financial resources. Do not assert that 'Nobody will utilize this type of table in the 21st century.' There will inevitably be individuals who find value in it, as personal preferences vary considerably among individuals.

Conversely, when constructing a dwelling, it is advisable not to discard any remaining materials, regardless of their size, as they may prove to be valuable in the future. I acquired this knowledge of wealth from an individual who possesses substantial financial resources. He operates a commercial establishment where surplus construction materials are stored. I found that to be unexpected. I inquired, "Excuse me, sir, may I inquire as to your rationale for keeping these items in a secure location?" Based on the multitude of disparate sizes, it is my belief that they lack practical value. He offered a subtle smile and retorted, "You perceive, this is precisely the predicament encountered by individuals of ordinary means and limited resources: a tendency to squander materials indiscriminately." Every skilled artisan possesses the knowledge of crafting something from the items you have disregarded as 'worthless'. In fact, I had the privilege of witnessing numerous instances where such items were successfully repurposed. Therefore, I strongly advise against discarding your possessions unless they are irreparably damaged.

Exemplary Strategies That Illuminate The Path To Wealth

This compendium elucidates the strategies and elusive elements underlying the millionaire mindset, providing insight into the individuals who possess the prowess to amass substantial affluence. Nothing comes easy so bear in mind that following these top-notch techniques and secrets does not give you an immediate result, rather when you think on them over and over and you put them into practice, you will begin to notice adjustments in your behavior and belief system. The pursuit of financial prosperity is within closer reach than one may fathom, provided that an individual possesses the requisite understanding, fortitude, and conscientiousness.

Millionaires embark on their journey from a state of unequivocal lucidity;

Being aware of your requirements is one aspect, comprehending your needs with utmost precision, right down to the minutest detail, is an entirely different matter. Wealthy individuals will consistently exhibit ambitions and aspirations characterized by meticulousness, diligently adhering to them until they achieve their desired objectives. This disposition is evident in accomplished athletes who meticulously plan and mentally envision their achievements long before they come to fruition. If one desires to cultivate a mindset of growth and prosperity, it is advisable to meticulously articulate one's specific requirements and gain a comprehensive understanding of the particulars well in advance, prior to their manifestation.

Millionaires never lose sight of their intention and goal under any circumstances.

In order to maintain focus on your intention and objective, it is imperative to consistently keep them at the forefront of your mind, thus ensuring that you do not divert your attention towards inconsequential matters. The most effective approach to accomplishing this objective is to cultivate a lifestyle in which you find yourself in the company of individuals who share the same aspirations as you. It is imperative not to disregard the smaller accomplishments one attains in order to maintain progress towards the primary objective.

- Millionaires possess a propensity for taking calculated risks. - Individuals with substantial wealth demonstrate a willingness to engage in risk-taking endeavors. - Those of considerable financial means exhibit a penchant for assuming risks. - Wealthy individuals exhibit a proclivity for venturing into risky propositions.

This distinctive mindset is recognized by all, and in order to achieve success, it is imperative to undertake calculated risks.

When one becomes aware of a substantial mistake made, and subsequently recognizes the potential for learning and personal growth derived from such an error, there is a reduction in the apprehension associated with undertaking risks.

Millionaires ascertain the precise factors that hold significance in their life.

The individual of considerable wealth comprehends that possessing liquid currency holds significant value in one's existence. Focusing on public opinion and rumors instead of pursuing financial success is unlikely to be in one's best interest. Your mental attitude and inner self possess the ability to exert a compelling force on you, propelling you toward achievement and contentment when you possess a clear understanding of your priorities.

Millionaires acknowledge their driving factors

Individuals have the potential to amass considerable financial gain when they are driven by negative motivations, thereby succumbing to unfavorable emotions and engaging in actions such as anger, greed, and so forth. To grasp such actions and emotions, yet none of these adverse endeavors and sentiments ultimately yield the purpose or attainment you seek. When the display of ardor and inspiration endears you to fulfill the needs of others, you will find that financial success is likewise accompanied by a sense of accomplishment. Ensure that you possess the appropriate driving factors that guide you towards financial prosperity.

"◻ Millionaire acknowledges the value of time

The wealthy individual comprehends the significance and worth of time, which is why they refrain from squandering it on unproductive activities or pursuits. In contrast, the ordinary individual typically exhibits a careless approach towards time management, often engaging in pastimes such as video games, television, social media, incessant phone usage, and trivial conversations, without recognizing their lack of substance or value. The affluent individual possesses a heightened awareness of his time, as all his actions are directed towards the attainment of his objective.

The mindset of individuals who possess great wealth recognizes the importance of being generous and contributing more than what is received.

The mindset of a person of wealth comprehends the significance and worthiness of philanthropy, consequently leading to an increased propensity for giving. In order to amass wealth, one must engage in social interactions, cultivate fruitful relationships, and possess valuable assets or skills. Without seeking reciprocity, endeavor to offer solutions to prevailing issues, for all other matters shall seamlessly align.

Millionaires consistently recognize the significance of upholding integrity.

This particular element holds paramount significance within the mindset conducive to achieving financial success. Many individuals are unaware that their lack of wealth stems from a compromised level of integrity, potentially on a subconscious level. Frequently, it is assumed that in order to attain monetary prosperity, it is necessary to relinquish one's sense of self, leading to behaviors that challenge our ethical principles. Attaining exceptional personal character characterized by utmost ethical rectitude does not necessitate possessing any kind of wealth or monetary resources. It is important to emphasize that not only can you generate financial prosperity, but you can also contribute to the welfare of those in your vicinity. Please make certain that as you ascend the path of prosperity, your moral rectitude remains beyond reproach.

Millionaires place trust in their subconscious beliefs. Millionaires have faith in their subconscious notions. Millionaires hold confidence in their subconscious convictions.

The conscious mind, at times, exhibits a lack of reliability, thus persistently altering its perspective on matters presented to it. The mindset of a millionaire necessitates a long-term orientation, thus transcending momentary emotions. This mindset, often referred to as intuition, extends beyond anxieties and apprehensions. However, some individuals may contend that they place trust in their subconscious thoughts to steer them towards the correct path and opportune moments.

How To Effectively Manage Your Finances? An Overview

Effective financial management is a crucial life skill that empowers individuals to attain their desired financial objectives. Irrespective of the amount of income one accrues, the ability to effectively administer and oversee one's finances is imperative in order to cultivate sustainable prosperity in the long run. To attain your financial objectives, it is imperative to possess the knowledge and skill of prudent money management. There exists a diverse array of applications accessible in the market that facilitate effortless management of personal finances, or alternatively, one has the option to seek the guidance of a financial advisor for expert assistance in money management. They will develop a financial strategy tailored to your income, debt level, financial objectives, investment time frame, and retirement plans. This article aims to provide insights into effective strategies for financial management, recommendations for prudent money management, and guidance specifically tailored for managing finances in India.

What is money management?

Upon embarking on your financial journey, it is imperative to familiarize yourself with the art of money management. Financial management entails the practice of budgeting, saving funds, diligently monitoring expenditures, adeptly managing taxes, and engaging in investment activities. The primary goal of financial management is to devise strategies that effectively minimize unnecessary expenditures, while directing resources towards items and investments that enhance one's overall quality of life and long-term financial growth.

Money management may vary among individuals due to variations in their income levels, lifestyles, ages, family dynamics, and other pertinent factors. By employing proper financial management techniques, you have the ability to attain your desired financial objectives.

What strategies can be employed to effectively manage personal finances? Money Management Suggestions

Develop a financial plan: The initial measure towards effective management of finances involves developing a comprehensive budget. Budgeting entails the process of approximating the monetary resources required to satisfy one's necessities, desires, and savings. Having a projected budget will enable you to exercise enhanced financial management. One may opt to utilize the 50/30/20 budgeting rule in order to avoid making excuses when it comes to budgeting. It enables individuals to allocate 50% of their earnings towards essential expenses, allocate 30% towards discretionary expenditures, and reserve 20% for savings and investment purposes. Suppose your monthly earnings amount to Rs. 1,00,000. According to this rule, it is advisable to allocate approximately Rs. 50,000 towards essential expenditures such as purchasing groceries, fulfilling rent obligations, and covering essential utilities. An amount of Rs. 30,000 can be allocated towards discretionary expenses such as dining out, travel, and entertainment, while the remaining Rs. 20,000 can be allocated towards investment opportunities in financial instruments, such as stocks, mutual funds, ETFs, or bonds.

Monitor your expenses: It is essential to monitor your expenses in order to obtain a precise assessment of your spending patterns. One can conduct a thorough examination of their various accounts, encompassing both debit and credit cards. Furthermore, it is possible to avail oneself of applications that are readily obtainable in the market, which facilitate the monitoring and subsequent mitigation of extravagant spending patterns. Prior to making any expenditure, it is prudent to evaluate whether the item in question is a necessity or a mere desire. In the case of it being a want, it is advisable to abstain from purchasing it.

Exercise prudent credit management: Possessing commendable credit management skills will enhance your eligibility for procuring loans during times of financial need. It is advised to refrain from surpassing 30% of your credit limit, as exceeding this threshold may have consequences on your credit score and can create disturbances within your budget. On the other hand, timely payments can aid in the establishment of a favorable credit score. Therefore, endeavor to utilize a credit card exclusively when the situation mandates it. The imposition of elevated interest rates on loans can substantially deplete one's savings, while the occurrence of delayed payments can result in the imposition of penalties. In order to circumvent incurring the penalty, it is advisable that you promptly settle your outstanding debt. Clearing your debt not only mitigates the accumulation of interest and outstanding loan obligations, but also safeguards your finances by preventing interest payments.

Enhance your knowledge on personal finance and investment: Acquiring a comprehensive understanding of personal finance has the potential to substantially enhance your financial circumstances, empowering you to make informed financial choices . Effective personal financial management enables individuals to skillfully handle monetary resources in various facets of their lives, thereby bolstering the inflow of funds. Individuals of all ages, regardless of their income or profession, have the capacity to acquire knowledge in the area of personal finance. You should allocate a portion of your schedule to engaging in literature or enrolling in web-based educational programs pertaining to personal finance and investment, in order to assert authority over your financial prospects.

Establish your retirement fund: Upon retirement, the cessation of a salary or consistent income will necessitate the need to maintain one's customary expenses. To secure your daily expenditures and ensure financial stability during your post-retirement phase, it is essential to proactively strategize your retirement plans without delay. Commence the process of accumulating and investing funds in a judicious manner, with the objective of establishing a retirement portfolio that prioritizes stability and caution. Consider options such as balanced mutual funds or large cap mutual funds for preservation of financial autonomy in your forthcoming years. Additionally, you may also explore investment alternatives, such as the Public Provident Fund (PPF) and the National Pension Scheme (NPS). The objective is to conservatively maintain and enhance your financial assets over a standard period of time.

Establish your contingency fund: A contingency fund refers to reserved financial resources intended to address unforeseen or sudden expenditures. It is imperative that the fund be maintained in a liquid state, as liquidity facilitates the prompt conversion of funds based on your desired timeframe. You have the option of directing your funds towards liquid funds or money market instruments. The main objective of the emergency fund is to safeguard or preserve your capital. It is advisable to maintain an emergency fund that encompasses 9-12 times your monthly income, given the inherent uncertainty surrounding the duration of potential job searches. Additionally, it is crucial to recognize that savings and emergency funds should be kept as distinct entities. It is advisable to allocate a portion of your monthly savings, approximately 10-20%, towards the establishment of an emergency fund. One can establish their emergency fund by distributing 25-30% in cash holdings, allocating 30% to gold (in either physical or digital form), and directing 40% toward debt instruments. Alternatively, one may choose to distribute their emergency funds into a specifically designated high-yield savings account, viewing the fund as a safeguard against unforeseen expenditures.

Effectively handle your taxation: Prioritize expanding your knowledge on taxation matters in advance of receiving your initial remuneration. It is imperative that you possess knowledge pertaining to income tax and possess a comprehensive understanding of its functionality. It will aid you in determining the amount of taxes incurred, as well as understanding the procedures for claiming deductions. Tax deductions can be obtained by allocating investments towards tax-saving instruments in accordance with section 80C of the income tax legislation in India, yielding considerable monetary savings.

Commence investing at an early stage: The sooner you initiate your investment portfolio, the greater the accrued interest on your investments. You receive interest on the accumulated interest from your investment, a concept commonly known as the phenomenon of compounding. Despite a restricted financial situation, one can initiate their investment endeavor by commencing a systematic investment plan (SIP) in mutual funds or index funds. Consistent investment will assist in fostering disciplined spending practices.

Maintain insurance coverage for personal safeguarding: It is imperative to proactively equip oneself with protective measures against unforeseen circumstances, such as health-related emergencies. Insurance policies such as health insurance, term insurance, and critical illness insurance serve to safeguard your family against potential financial turmoil. It will facilitate the provision of financial assistance for hospitalization, sickness, or medical treatment to your beloved individuals.

Establishing financial objectives: Setting financial objectives aids in preventing excessive spending and maintaining a concentrated approach. Your financial objective may encompass the acquisition of a residential property, the establishment of a marital union, or the provision of education for your children. Therefore, according to your financial objectives, you strategize your budget, savings, and investment plans.

How To Save? 30 Easy Tricks

The upward trend in the average expenditure associated with the cost of living, which is further exacerbated by the global geopolitical landscape, is prompting a considerable number of Italians to seek strategies for reducing their expenses. There exist numerous highly effective strategies that can be employed to save significant amounts of money each year. Within this article, we will present you with a comprehensive list of 30 excellent approaches that allow for substantial financial gains through the practice of saving.

The monetary resource in question, on which guidance is provided herein, is segmented into six distinct classifications:

general savings tips;

Strategies for minimizing expenses while shopping

Strategies for maximizing savings at a financial institution

How to promote financial conservation within the household.

Methods to achieve cost savings in healthcare

Methods for cost reduction in residential properties.

Presented herein are comprehensive guidelines to adhere to in order to restrict excessive spending.

In order to achieve cost savings, it may suffice to alter certain behaviors. Please find below ten specific instances:

1. Create an emergency fund

Low-income households equipped with a minimum of €1,000 in an emergency reserve exhibit greater financial resilience when compared to middle-income households, albeit with comparatively lower levels of savings.

2. Establish a budget

The initial procedure is straightforward: over the course of a month, diligently retain the tax receipts for all your purchases and categorize them accordingly based on shopping, dining out, personal grooming, and so forth. By the conclusion of the month, it will become evident as to how your finances have been allocated and in which areas potential savings can be made.

3. Adhere to the envelope budgeting technique.

If you encounter difficulty in excessive spending, consider utilizing the envelope system, wherein you allocate a predetermined amount for each designated spending category, allocating one envelope for each category. And once the funds contained within the envelope are expended, no further alternative method of payment can be utilized.

4. Think ahead

There exists a nuanced yet significant distinction between reducing expenditures and setting aside funds for future needs. It is imperative to consider the forthcoming months and years as well, and a prudent approach to achieve this objective is to retain the funds within a deposit account.

5. Save automatically

The process of automating savings represents a straightforward and highly efficient method of accumulating funds, as it ensures that any surplus money remains concealed and untouched. On a monthly basis, it is possible for your employer to allocate a specified portion of your salary by means of facilitating a transfer to a designated pension fund.

6. Set short-term savings goals

To commence, it would be ideal to establish a simplistic objective to pursue, such as allocating a weekly amount of 20 euros. Giving priority to the immediate future can yield tangible outcomes, particularly for individuals who are inexperienced in the practice of financial preservation.

7. Commence setting aside funds for your retirement at the earliest convenience.

Only a small number of individuals achieve substantial wealth solely through their personal income. Compound interest is the key contributor to the accumulation of wealth over an extended period of time. Due to the advantage of time being in their favor, younger employees are in the most advantageous position to allocate funds for their retirement.

8. Adhere to the 24-hour waiting period.

This regulation permits one to circumvent the acquisition of costly or superfluous items driven by impulsive tendencies.

Prior to making a purchase for which you have little or no genuine necessity, it is advisable to engage in a period of contemplation lasting no less than 24 hours.

. Indulge in self-pampering, while also utilizing this occasion to save.

Aggregate the expenses incurred from discretionary indulgences with your accumulated savings. For instance, in the event that you choose to indulge in the luxury of ice cream, allocate an equivalent sum towards your savings account. If you come to the realization that you are unable to set aside the equivalent amount, it indicates that the present moment is not suitable for indulging in impulsive desires.

10. Compute the value of your acquisitions based on the amount of time invested in employment.

Assess the cost of the item under consideration by juxtaposing it against your earnings on an hourly or daily basis. When considering a pair of shoes priced at 50 euros and taking into account your hourly wage of 10 euros, it is important to reflect on whether investing five hours of work justifies the purchase.

Expenditure related to food constitutes a substantial portion of the financial allocations for individuals and households. What strategies do you employ to effectively reduce expenditure on shopping?

11. Bring lunch to work

If dining at the workplace's bar or canteen comes at an approximate expense of 5 euros, opting to prepare one's own lunch at home can incur a cost that is at least half, presenting an opportunity to save over 500 euros annually.

12. Dining out on a monthly basis

In order to enhance your financial savings while maintaining your desired standard of living, initiate a reduction in the frequency of dining out.

13. Plan your shopping

Pre-plan your meals and adhere to your predetermined shopping list upon arrival at the grocery store. Numerous individuals succumb to temptation and engage in unnecessary expenditures by purchasing products that are not included on their list. Strategically arranging your grocery shopping at the supermarket can lead to substantial annual savings of hundreds of euros.

14. Please be mindful of the cost per kilogram.

Within the confines of the price tag displayed in supermarkets, in inconspicuous print, the cost of the merchandise is exhibited in terms of kilograms. This will facilitate the process of comparing and selecting the most suitable product, free from any influence based on its size.

An alternative method of saving involves scrutinizing your banking expenses to ensure that you are minimizing unnecessary expenditures, while being diligent in capitalizing on the most favorable terms and conditions available. Allow me to present the methods for reducing expenses on your checking account.

15. Please verify the accurate expenses associated with your credit card.

Make an effort to comprehend the true expenses associated with the selected credit card. Certain charges and commissions, particularly those of an annual nature, may escape scrutiny.

16. Use the ATM

It is recommended to utilize the ATM in order to avoid incurring fees that adversely affect your savings.

17. Make a withdrawal at the service desks of your bank.

If your bank imposes additional charges for withdrawing cash at non-affiliated bank branches, it is advisable to strategically manage your funds and ensure that you exclusively make withdrawals at the counter of your designated bank.

18. Check the conditions constantly

Pursuant to legal requirements, the bank is obligated to notify you in the event that the specified conditions for your account deteriorate, and consequently, you are entitled to terminate the contract without incurring any penalties.

19. Utilize the benefits of online banking

Conduct transactions such as wire transfers from the comfort of your home banking platform, by securely accessing and managing your online account through the prescribed procedures dictated by your bank. Digital transactions incur no fees, whereas in-person transactions frequently involve the assessment of commissions.

There are several straightforward strategies to comprehend, in collaboration with your family, how to economize on expenditures.

20. Establish a budgetary constraint for the procurement of presents.

Suggest the implementation of well-defined expenditure boundaries for familial gifts and/or the adoption of a system wherein individuals procure only a singular present for each family member throughout the Christmas season. These limitations have a tendency to decrease costs and are greatly valued by family members who possess fewer financial means.

21. Buy gifts in advance

This option provides an opportune opportunity for careful consideration of significant presents, typically pricier ones, and potentially purchasing them during discounted periods.

22. Don't buy cheap clothes

On occasion, it is logical to place an emphasis on the aspect of quality rather than price when acquiring clothing items for one's family. A shirt or coat that is priced affordably may not offer good value for older family members if it deteriorates within a year, but it may be a sensible choice for children, who outgrow their clothes rapidly. When selecting garments, we take into account various quality-related aspects such as the fabric composition, the sewing technique employed, the durability with respect to washing, among other factors.

23. Arrange a day of no expenditures.

Designate a "day of refraining from expenditure" during which each member of the family is prohibited from engaging in any personal consumption. Secure a memorable family evening at no cost by opting to dine at home and curate engaging activities indoors or in the great outdoors.

Health is of utmost importance, I must emphasize. In the event that visits are necessary, it is imperative that the fervent desire to economize should not serve as a hindrance. Nevertheless, adhering to a handful of beneficial practices can prevent exorbitant expenditures in regards to one's wellbeing.

24. Don't skip checkups

Regular dental examinations, for instance, serve as a proactive measure against the development of cavities, which not only incur substantial costs but also cause significant inconvenience during treatment.

25. Choose generic drugs

Please consult with your physician to determine which generic medications may be suitable for your individual needs. Opting for generic medications can yield substantial annual savings amounting to hundreds of dollars, when contrasted with the expenditure incurred on branded pharmaceuticals.

Whether it pertains to residential mortgage or the efficient administration of household expenditures, the following are guidelines to save significant amounts of euros within one's residence.

26. The transfer of liability for the loan

Are you aware that by means of subrogation, it is possible to transfer your mortgage from the bank with which you originally obtained it to a different institution, in order to renegotiate the fixed or variable interest rate? This may result in saving a substantial amount of money, potentially amounting to thousands of euros.

27. Watch out for bills

If you reside in a solitary or dual occupancy arrangement, it may be prudent to remunerate your electricity and gas expenditure exclusively on a consumption-based basis. Please reach out to your respective supplier companies to inquire about the ongoing promotional deals.

28. A weatherproof home

Ensure the well-being of your household by preventing the occurrence of apertures or crevices that allow the escape of warm air during winter and cool air during summer.

29. Use less water

Implement the installation of low-flow nozzles on faucets as a measure to minimize expenditure on water consumption.

30. Reduce the amount of detergent utilized in the washing machine.

The laundry detergent available for purchase at present is of immense concentration and potency. Utilize a reduced quantity relative to the prescribed amount specified on the packaging.

Strategies For Disregarding Advertisements

Promotion is the essence of trade and a vital element for every enterprise.

Henry Ford proclaimed that each penny allocated towards advertising constituted a momentous investment, and his assertion remains unequivocal.

Without advertising is impossible to get noticed on the market and you can't buy a product if you don't know that it exists. Internationally recognized corporations allocate substantial financial resources each month towards advertising endeavors, which entail engaging renowned Hollywood directors, esteemed actors, and highly compensated sports figures for the promotion of their products. These corporations strategize by creating compelling viral campaigns across various digital platforms and deploying eye-catching posters in prominent urban centers to generate widespread product awareness. With an effective advertising campaign, there is a significant likelihood of successful sales for every product.

However, advertising has the potential to be excessively intrusive and bothersome.

How to ignore advertising?

It appears to be a formidable undertaking, however, by employing certain strategies, we can overlook it.

On the World Wide Web, specialized software like AdBlock Plus can be utilized. This software application serves as a supplementary feature for the latest web browsers, namely Mozilla Firefox or Google Chrome, effectively preventing the occurrence of intrusive pop-up advertisements during internet browsing activities. Furthermore, it conceals a majority of the banner advertisements that are displayed on websites.

Numerous individuals exhibit aversion towards these programs due to their concealment of site advertisements, impeding the generation of revenue. Nonetheless, these same individuals deploy such programs as they find banners and pop-ups highly vexatious, frequently concealing unwanted malicious software and viruses.

To install the product, simply retrieve it from the Web Store or conduct a Google search to acquire it. It is accessible free of charge and does not impose any disruptions to your browsing or computer performance.

In regard to television advertising, there lie solely two viable options; the initial being the subscription to a premium television service wherein the quantity of advertisements is diminished, or alternatively, one may opt to switch channels during commercial intervals.

These solutions consist of two remedial measures that exhibit limited efficacy, yet they represent the sole available options for implementation.

In the context of telephone advertising (conducting promotional calls), you have the option to include the numbers of incoming calls on the blocklist of your smartphone, thereby deterring persistent and bothersome calls from familiar numbers. Should these numbers persist in their calls, it would be advisable to pursue legal action by engaging the services of law enforcement or seeking assistance from an attorney who specializes in consumer rights. This will allow for potential compensation and the possibility of initiating legal proceedings against the responsible entities.

However, the true efficacious solution for advertising lies in adopting the appropriate cognitive perspective, whereby one acknowledges our genuine necessities and recognizes that all else is superfluous.

Consider your monthly financial allocation and assess your expenditure limitations, thereby mitigating the impulse to purchase numerous advertised merchandise. Occasionally, engaging in such actions may be permissible; however, exercising caution is paramount, as shielding oneself from succumbing to the influence of advertisers is crucial.

One need not hold the belief that advertising is detrimental; on the contrary, it is indispensable for commerce as it enables numerous businesses to generate revenue and effectively promote their offerings to potential customers. Advertisers are diligently fulfilling their professional obligations by skillfully crafting slogans, skits, and songs that generate lasting mental impressions and serve as powerful stimuli for consumer purchases.

Ultimately, it pertains solely to matters of commerce, and if you perceive it as a conflict, your perspective is incorrect. It is imperative that you maintain a conscious recognition of your desired choices and refrain from being swayed by advertising stimuli. You will be under no obligation to purchase a product unless you so choose, independent of any influence from advertising.

Strategies For Overcoming Impulsive Shopping Patterns

Purchasing goods is not inherently negative; it is justifiable to acquire the items we desire and require. Moreover, it serves as a meaningful psychological motivator to dedicate oneself to one's labor, and the gratification of acquiring an item following diligent effort and sacrifice is truly satisfying. It can be regarded as a well-deserved reward for our hard work and unwavering dedication.

However, it is essential to exercise caution in order to avoid excessive indulgence. Compulsive shopping can give rise to significant financial and familial consequences.

What is compulsive shopping?

In brief, it refers to the uncontrolled and irrepressible inclination that drives individuals to purchase a multitude of items that are unnecessary, unused, or not of personal relevance. However, at that particular juncture, we are unavoidably compelled to make the purchase.

Why?

This condition refers to a psychological disorder characterized by an individual experiencing gratification or pleasure derived from the act of purchasing items. The joy is ephemeral and the only way to experience it again is by purchasing something fresh. Additionally, the individual experiences a sense of affluence and authority, completely devoid of any predicaments.

In the most extreme instances, this disorder may give rise to kleptomania, characterized by the compulsion to purloin items solely for the emotional satisfaction derived from such illicit acts.

This issue necessitates the implementation of a medical professional's prescribed treatment plan, medication aimed at mood regulation, and participation in group therapy sessions.

However, I am able to propose a few solutions that can mitigate impulsive buying tendencies.

The initial approach entails abstaining from carrying cash, or only carrying the essential amount required for transactions. This habit is anticipated to have an impact on the monthly budget and poses a significant hindrance to making purchases, as there is a limited amount of funds available.

Nevertheless, an individual with a compulsion may employ a credit card for making purchases, particularly in online transactions. This leads us to the subsequent approach, whereby the individual's credit card is confiscated and substituted with a prepaid card that needs to be recharged following each purchase. Consequently, individuals will be compelled to expend additional time on recharging the prepaid card and withdrawing funds from their monthly financial allocation. By means of this strategy, only the most essential purchases will be included in the closure process.

I have experimented with this system initially, and I can attest to its efficacy. By employing this method, I managed to effectively curtail my online shopping activities, resulting in substantial financial savings.

The proposed solution is elementary and slightly rudimentary. The initial step to address this predicament entails acknowledging the existence of the issue and promptly seeking expert assistance. This matter bears a striking resemblance to the phenomenon of gambling addiction and has the potential to yield adverse outcomes for the entire household and financial stability.

Acknowledge the existence of this issue and recognizing the importance of seeking assistance constitutes the initial phase in resolving it (a principle applicable to all aspects of life). Conversely, disregarding the problem will merely exacerbate it and give rise to significantly graver repercussions.

The validity of your budget and the sacrifices made to adhere to it may be rendered void due to this issue. This conflict is of utmost significance; are you committed to achieving victory, or do you prefer to squander valuable time and persist in the superfluous accumulation of items each day?

The upcoming conflict poses immense challenges; nevertheless, it is imperative that victory be achieved through any means necessary.

Essentials of Monetary Governance and Attaining Economic Autonomy

Attaining a state of fiscal security and liberation, unburdened by apprehensions, tensions, or anxieties related to money, is an attainable goal for individuals regardless of their financial history or socioeconomic standing. Indeed, attaining financial independence and prosperity simply entails mastering one's financial affairs, necessitating the acquisition and cultivation of what is commonly known as "the art of financial management."

Proficient money management abilities are of utmost importance for achieving long-term fiscal stability and autonomy. Lack of these skills and the requisite understanding to apply them may result in an unfavorable financial situation, potentially characterized by financial limitations, burdensome debts, living from one paycheck to another, unattained financial aspirations, and detrimental financial practices.

It is imperative to comprehend that the journey towards achieving financial independence is characterized by a circuitous and extensive route, frequently accompanied by fiscal obstacles, trade-offs, obligations, and strains. Moreover, it is crucial to acknowledge that the pace at which we navigate this route is unique to each individual, contingent upon their economic standing, financial objectives, and various other factors.

Having mentioned that, the path towards achieving financial independence remains largely uniform among individuals.

Regardless of your identity, financial history, or present economic situation, embarking on the journey towards financial independence and achievement merely requires understanding the principles of money management. This can be accomplished by breaking it down into the following basic steps:

The initial phase involves fostering a comprehensive and profound comprehension of your financial situation. One cannot assume control over something one lacks knowledge of. In order to effectively govern your finances and make steady progress towards attaining financial independence and achievement, it is crucial to gain comprehensive knowledge about the sources and amounts of your income, as well as how you allocate and utilize it. This entails a comprehensive understanding of your financial standing, including the loans you are repaying, your financial aspirations, and other pertinent factors. Gaining a thorough comprehension of your financial situation holds significant weight in effectively managing your money and achieving financial independence. Failing to undertake this crucial step is akin to piloting Flight-Financial-Freedom without proper visibility, with a lack of knowledge about the available resources and the trajectory of the journey.

The next fundamental measure towards achieving proficient money management and attaining financial autonomy involves the meticulous monitoring and oversight of your financial resources on a daily, weekly, monthly, and yearly basis. Effective money management can be understood as the competent handling of one's finances in a manner consistent with their present lifestyle and conducive to accomplishing their financial objectives in the short, medium, and long term. After acquiring a comprehensive understanding of your financial situation and clearly defining your financial objectives, the task of managing your finances will become considerably more manageable.

The third and ultimate phase of proficient financial management entails the fostering of financial autonomy through the practice of purposeful savings. This entails saving with a distinct investment objective in mind, such as directing funds towards valuable investment assets like life insurance, an emergency fund, real estate acquisition, entrepreneurial pursuits, or participation in the stock market.

Individuals who have attained both financial success and freedom have accomplished such through the application of these three fundamental measures. Beneath the primary procedures lie a sequence of subordinate procedures and financial elements that necessitate your knowledge and comprehension in order to adeptly assume the role of a personal finance executor.

The primary objective of this guide is to provide you with practical insights necessary for effectively executing the three core principles of financial management. By doing so, you can initiate your journey towards achieving financial independence and prosperity.

Consider this guide as a comprehensive blueprint to achieve financial success and attain personal freedom.

A Three-Stage Methodology

Firstly, comprehend your financial situation

In order to attain financial independence, a comprehensive and multi-dimensional strategy is imperative. This is due to the fact that financial independence comprises a multitude of interconnected objectives, which collectively culminate in the ultimate aim of achieving complete financial freedom.

However, in order to embark upon this journey, it is imperative to acquire the art of financial management. As previously mentioned, the very first stride in this direction is gaining a comprehensive understanding of your financial situation. This implies that it is imperative for you to have a comprehensive understanding of various financial aspects, such as your income, expenditure patterns, financial obligations including loans and mortgages, income stability, saving habits and objectives, as well as your investment aspirations like initiating a business venture or purchasing stocks.

Prior to embarking on the pursuit of becoming an adept personal financial manager or attaining financial independence, it is imperative to first establish a solid comprehension of your financial circumstances and overall monetary situation. By attaining a comprehensive understanding of one's finances, one can effectively attain dominion over them and proficiently administer them, thus allowing for the attainment of a sense of tranquility and security regarding one's financial well-being.

Strategies for Fostering Financial Consciousness in Your Existence

In the context of this guide, the phrase financial awareness signifies a condition of conscious and comprehensive understanding regarding crucial aspects of one's financial circumstances, including but not limited to their earnings, expenditure patterns, debts, financial obligations and objectives, saving practices, investment ambitions, legacy aspirations, as well as short, medium, and long-term financial strategies and objectives.

"You can foster this state through:

#: Taking stock

In order to proficiently administer your finances, it is imperative to comprehensively evaluate your current financial status and strive to acquire a profound knowledge of every aspect pertaining to your financial resources.

What is your per pay period income? What portion of this amount is allocated towards tax payments and other monthly contributions? In relation to the remaining net income, how do your consumption patterns impact your allocation of funds? What are your immediate, intermediate, and long-range financial objectives and what actions do you need to take in order to attain them?

Pose these inquiries to yourself, along with their corresponding related prompts, in order to attain a more comprehensive understanding of your current financial standing and your desired financial position within a specified timeframe.

Here, it is imperative that you devote careful consideration to several pivotal components:

Your total and net earnings: Your total earnings represent the amount of income owed to you prior to the deduction of taxes and other monthly withholdings. This information can be obtained by referring to your paystub or your bank statement. The net income holds greater significance compared to the gross income, as it represents the remaining funds at the end of each month after deducting federal and state tax payments, in addition to withholdings for obligations like FICA and Medicare.

Your monthly outlays: Also referred to as monthly overheads, your monthly outlays denote the sum of money disbursed on a regular basis, encompassing various components such as lodging/mortgage, transportation, attire, amusement, cable, and an array of both essential and non-essential expenses. One can ascertain their monthly expenses by conducting an analysis of their bank statement, comparing the data from month to month. Alternatively, if one predominately relies on cash for transactions, they can meticulously monitor and document each occurrence of financial expenditure throughout a specified payment cycle.

PLEASE TAKE NOTE: In this context, it is crucial to allocate special attention to your 'monthly expenditure,' a financial term denoting the fundamental sum of money required each month to cover essential expenses such as shelter, sustenance, clothing, and other basic necessities.

The determination of your monthly expenses holds significant relevance as it underpins the fundamental principles of prudent financial management and the attainment of fiscal independence. In essence, in order to effectively administer your finances, it is essential that you maintain a lifestyle that is below your means, enabling you to save and invest judiciously. Consequently, it becomes imperative to establish the foundational amount of funds required each month to sustain a satisfactory standard of living.

Consideration of your liabilities and assets: It is important to recognize the distinction between good and bad debt, particularly focusing on the latter which arises from unfavorable spending patterns, such as unnecessary credit card expenditures. Debt holds considerable significance in your financial affairs as it bears substantial influence on your monthly outlay. Moreover, it plays a decisive role in determining your net worth, which is derived from the difference between your assets and liabilities. Please ensure to duly acknowledge your financial obligations, including your mortgage, credit card debt, car loan, student loan, and any other outstanding debts. The significance of these two figures, namely your indebtedness and your total assets, should not be undermined, as it is worth acknowledging that by diminishing your debt burden, you consequently augment your net worth and enhance your overall financial well-being.

Based on the aforementioned information, the task of discerning one's financial position and, of greater significance, comprehending the necessary steps towards becoming a more proficient financial steward and embarking upon the journey towards fiscal independence should become more lucid.

Achieving financial independence is a consequence of adhering to a lifestyle of frugality, diligently setting aside a portion of your income, and strategically allocating your savings into lucrative investment opportunities. It is advisable to focus on investments that yield a passive income stream, requiring minimal active involvement on your part.

After conducting a comprehensive assessment, make a notation of whether your monthly expenditures surpass your net income. This scenario indicates that you are exceeding your financial capabilities, thereby increasing the likelihood of accruing debt, facing substantial financial burdens, living paycheck to paycheck, and diminishing your prospects of attaining financial independence, particularly if you continue to maintain your current circumstances.

In such a scenario, the concept of "managing your finances efficiently" entails making a conscientious determination to adopt a lifestyle that is conducive to spending less than your income. This will necessitate making challenging financial choices or implementing measures that may require sacrifice, such as channeling funds into an emergency fund and a savings or investment account, as well as strategically paying off outstanding debts.

Action step

Comprehending your finances ultimately entails the ability to confidently ascertain both your monthly net income and, more significantly, how you allocate and utilize these funds.

In order to achieve this, it is recommended that you monitor your monthly income and expenditures. One may opt to carry out this task manually, alternatively, they could consult their bank statement. Additionally, various auxiliary resources such as spreadsheets or smartphone applications may be utilized for the same purpose.

The principal notion entails attaining a comprehensive understanding of one's present fiscal situation, enabling the formulation of a comprehensive strategy to effectively administer one's finances, thereby gradually ascending the path to financial independence.

This transitions us to the subsequent phase in the realm of monetary control and attaining fiscal independence:

What Are The Reasons For The Crucial Significance Of Financial Intelligence?

Financial acumen is of utmost importance for each individual's sustenance, particularly amidst the prevailing economic downturn. We are frequently exposed to this statement, yet it seems that a significant portion of the population lacks a clear understanding of its meaning. Our unawareness also prevents us from gaining the essential learning that is obligatory for it.

Financial acumen entails possessing the knowledge and ability to make informed decisions regarding finances, thereby mitigating the likelihood of encountering fiscal challenges. It is as fundamental as that.

Generally, it is requisite for individuals to incur expenses, and the issue at hand pertains to the availability of ample or inadequate funds. Individuals, households, and enterprises of various scales grapple with these challenges on a daily basis. When considering this matter, how do you proceed? What steps would you take to obtain the opportunity to address the matter? A prerequisite for successfully navigating any financial challenges that may arise in your life is to possess a strong foundation of financial acumen.

Assets refer to the tangible or intangible holdings that generate financial gains or income. Conversely, debts pertain to the financial obligations you owe to others or any liabilities that result in the reduction of funds within your possession.

It is imperative that you possess a comprehensive understanding of all liabilities, assets, cash flows, and other related factors. Due to its capacity to foster an understanding of one's financial predicament and any transaction requiring one's participation. Every instance you are in need of acquiring offers, real estate, or embarking on an investment or business venture, it is imperative to possess a strong level of financial acumen. Inculcating financial acumen prompts one to meticulously evaluate opportunities and effectively manage savings. This fosters the necessity for individuals to possess a considerable comprehension of their financial affairs, given the gravity of statistical information. If one lacks knowledge of their present location, how can they determine the appropriate course towards their desired destination? Furthermore, the cultivation of financial acumen enhances one's confidence. As you enhance your financial acumen, you elevate your earnings, adeptly manage your expenses, augment your assets, and employ indebtedness judiciously rather than further accumulating it.

Chapter Two: Principles of Individual Financial Management

The Principle of Giving

One does not necessitate a religious inclination to recognize that the act of providing for and serving others is esteemed as a commendable trait, while immaturity is generally regarded as an unfavorable characteristic. Self-centeredness is a customary and inherent trait, however, conversely, it is capricious and largely gives rise to unhappiness (consider the examples of the Grinch and Mr. Scrooge).

As young individuals, we are taught the value of sharing, and it is imperative that this principle of giving endures throughout our adult lives. Engaging in acts of generosity enhances your moral disposition. It enhances one's personal development as an individual of the male gender. It elicits heightened sensations of joy.

I would suggest that your generous donations be categorized proportionally to your income level. When the act of giving is somewhat challenging for you, it tends to yield a more solidly positive result in terms of benefiting others. Therefore, as your income experiences growth over time, it follows that the amount you contribute should also increase. Selecting a rate as your primary goal will ensure that. This particular standard has been in existence for a significant number of years - the term "tithing" is defined as the act of giving a tenth of one's income or possessions.

Financial resources are attracted to individuals who exhibit responsible and prudent behavior towards them, while those who demonstrate negligence or mismanagement experience a divergence of such resources.

Cash typically accumulates when it is understood and valued. By comprehending the impact that money can have on one's life and recognizing its significance, you will be in an advantageous position.

It is not intended to suggest that you ought to have an affection for money, as you should refrain from doing so. In any event, it is crucial to acknowledge the role it plays in our lives. Regardless, cash matters. When you consider that factor and base your decisions on that comprehension, your finances will become more manageable.

Limit the amount of debt allocated to income-generating assets.

With Visas and auto credits, each penny you spend to reimburse that obligation is cash flushed down the depletion. All except a few select automobile models undergo a complete decay to value zero, necessitating additional expenses for repairs and financial charges that surpass reasonable expectations for potential return upon resale to the owner. Morris elucidates, "The exorbitant interest rates associated with utilizing credit cards to purchase household goods and clothing items that depreciate rapidly are disadvantageous financial transactions." If you happen to find yourself in debt, it is advisable to focus on financing assets that have a long-term value retention, such as real estate and education."

Commence engaging in combat from an early stage of life.

Acknowledge that the total amount of your savings is determined by both the interest you accumulate on those savings and the duration of time over which you save.

Do not obtain funds that you are unable to reimburse.

Be a conscientious borrower who repays as promised, proving yourself worthy of obtaining credit in the future. Prior to proceeding with your acquisition, it is recommended that you evaluate your total payment obligations and assess your income availability to meet these financial commitments.

Understanding the Temporal Value of Currency

When one consistently remains inactive for a prolonged period, one tends to overlook this fundamental principle: the importance of the time value of money.

The passage of time can either be advantageous or detrimental to your finances. It is proving advantageous in your speculations but detrimental in fulfilling your obligations. Believe it or not, even that dollar stashed beneath your mattress is experiencing a gradual erosion of its value. Please exercise caution when placing trust in me. Observe the Consumer Price Index over the past few years. Prices are steadily rising, causing the value of your mattress dollar to progressively diminish.

However, time is not typically burdensome; rather, it often invigorates as well. As an illustration, in the event that an individual were to make a monthly investment of $200 over a duration of ten years, with the amount growing at a compounded annual rate of 10%, the total sum accumulated at the conclusion of said period would exceed $1.25 million dollars. Over the course of those 40 years, your contributions would amount to $96,000. The remaining balance of $1.25 million dollars, apart from the initial contribution, represents accumulated interest as well as a significant period of time.

Please make every effort to submit your contribution at the earliest possible opportunity.

The paramount financial challenge faced by all individuals is the endeavor of saving funds for retirement. It represents the most substantial sum of money that you must endeavor to accumulate throughout your existence, and the only reliable means to accomplish this objective is through consistent savings over an extended duration. Regardless, should you commence saving at an early stage in your professional journey, the prospect becomes less daunting.

Practicing frugality during one's early years allows one to harness the power of compounding. In the event that Person A were to receive an annual amount of $5,000 from the age of 25 to 40, accumulating to a total of $75,000, followed by the cessation of any further contributions, and Person B were to consistently contribute $5,000 annually from the age of 40 to 65, totaling $125,000 in contributions, assuming a growth rate of 5%, it can be deduced that Person A will accumulate over $400,000 by retirement, whereas Person B will only possess $256,000. This discrepancy arises primarily due to the fact that Person A initiated their savings earlier, despite setting aside a smaller amount.

According to Storjohann, "Commencing your contributions earlier allows for a longer exposure of your money in the market, potentially generating returns beyond inflation and securing a steady income stream for retirement." You are currently entering a phase of significant growth and development for the next 30-35 years, during which it is crucial for your financial resources to flourish. This is because, at the age of 65, we will rely on our accumulated assets to sustain us in the form of replacement income. We are in the process of creating a substantial collective fund that will provide us with a dependable source of income for the entirety of our remaining years.

If you aspire to enhance the ease of saving for retirement, it is advisable to commence without delay, if you have not already done so. Your mind is likely occupied with justifications at this moment – how desperately you need the money immediately, how you will start once you acquire it, how you can access it later – however, the reality remains that there will always be an excuse. Upon receiving a salary increase, it may be necessary for you to allocate funds towards a future home purchase, or alternatively, plan for the expenses associated with a wedding, starting a family, or even saving for their education. There will never be an opportune moment to commence setting aside funds for retirement. You will consistently be required to do it amidst competing priorities. Therefore, ascertain the method to accomplish it temporarily as various demands on your life surface. Upon reaching the age of 65 and entering retirement, you will undoubtedly find immense satisfaction in the fact that you possess sufficient financial resources to sustain a comfortable lifestyle for the ensuing few decades. Should you fail to do so, there is a possibility that, upon reaching the age of 55, you may experience a reduction in workforce and face financial constraints with respect to your retirement savings, which may lead to regret and dissatisfaction towards your past actions.

Understanding Credit

An increasing number of individuals are currently finding themselves trapped in a distressing situation of financial indebtedness. Moreover, even if your credit is immaculate, it is difficult to disregard the incessant advertising, promotional campaigns, and offerings for credit restoration prominently showcased on television, radio, and in various print media. To be candid, issues with credit are currently reaching epidemic proportions. Poised as customary components of adulthood, student loans, credit cards, and medical bills collectively emanate an air of normalcy. Nevertheless, this assertion was not consistently accurate in the past, and moreover, it need not necessarily hold true for you.

If you have chosen to peruse this book due to circumstances involving compromised credit or indebtedness, it is imperative to realize that no situation is irreversibly bleak. Regardless of your credit score, there are methods available to enhance it. It might require a considerable amount of time and diligent effort; nevertheless, there is potential for improvement. If you are perusing this book in an effort to proactively evade credit complications down the line, you have positioned yourself a step ahead in this endeavor.

In order to effectively address and rectify a negative credit situation, it is imperative to acquire comprehensive knowledge pertaining to the concept of credit and its consequences on one's financial standing. Credit refers to the capacity of an entity or individual to obtain goods or services in advance of settling the associated financial obligations. Evidently, credit cards can be categorized accordingly. However, any contractual arrangements you enter into with an establishment that offers commodities or services will ultimately contribute to or negatively impact your creditworthiness. Various utilities, such as electricity, gas, internet, and cable services, will all impact your credit. Furthermore, the creditworthiness of individuals can be impacted by various financial arrangements such as car loans, bank loans, mortgages, student loans, and any other form of contractual commitment whereby a service is provided and payment is deferred to a later point in time.

Likewise, a credit rating represents an assessment of your capacity to meet financial obligations, drawn from your past interactions with credit providers. When submitting an application for a loan, a new bank account, or on certain occasions, even employment opportunities, it is customary for an entity to assess your credit record. Your credit record shall indicate any occurrences of delayed payments, as well as the presence of any outstanding or defaulted debts. For certain lenders, these occurrences can potentially impede access to future loans or credit. In alternative scenarios, while these indicators may not serve as impediments to obtaining credit, they will incur additional costs by raising the interest rates applicable to a loan or reducing the extent of credit available to you.

Nevertheless, your credit status does not present a straightforward picture, as it does not exclusively encompass the balance of your debts and the payments you have made. Your creditworthiness is determined not only by a credit score, but also by a credit report. Your credit report serves as a comprehensive account of your prior credit-related transactions, encompassing elements such as loans, invoices, credit card usage, and more. Three credit bureaus are responsible for maintaining credit reports. The aforementioned entities include Experian, Transunion, and

Equifax. In addition to the information provided in your credit report, you possess a credit score.

A credit score is a numerical assessment employed to ascertain your ability to effectively handle financial commitments, which is derived from evaluating your prior credit history. The credit bureaus Experian, Transunion, and Equifax leverage data obtained from your credit report in order to determine your credit score. There are multiple variables that contribute to the assessment of your credit score. The manner in which you have fulfilled your financial obligations, specifically in terms of debt repayment, constitutes 35% of your credit score. This constitutes the greatest proportion of your credit score and holds paramount significance. Instances of delayed payments and defaults will be classified under this classification. If you consistently make timely payments and maintain a record of at least paying the minimum balance on your debts, this will have a positive impact on this aspect of your credit rating. The subsequent significant component involved in the computation of your credit score is the aggregate amount of debt you possess. Nevertheless, it is not merely a straightforward calculation of your outstanding debt, but rather a measurement of the proportion between your indebtedness and your available credit. The debt-to-credit ratio holds significant importance as it comprises 30% of your credit score, a weightage marginally lower than that of your payment history.

The remaining variables that contribute to the determination of your credit score encompass the duration of your credit history, the diversity of your credit accounts, and the instances of credit inquiries. The duration of your credit history contributes to 15% of your credit score. This factor may occasionally disadvantage inexperienced individuals who are new to the credit industry, although it is not inherently accurate to generalize. Individuals who had the opportunity to establish a credit history during their adolescent and early adult years may find themselves in a more advantageous position compared to those in their forties or fifties who exclusively relied on cash transactions throughout their lives, thus failing to build a credit record.

The subsequent factor pertains to the variety of disparate credit accounts in your possession. This factor contributes to 10% of your credit score. Therefore, in a scenario where an individual possesses a minimal number of loans, and the majority of their credit is constituted by credit cards and utilities, the calculation of their credit score will vary when compared to a situation where the bulk of their credit is rooted in loans. The final determinant is the quantity of credit inquiries displayed on your report, constituting 10% of your credit score. Credit inquiries may originate from various sources. The addition of a new line of credit will be reflected consistently on your credit report. Furthermore, every instance in which you personally access and review your credit score will be reflected on your credit report. Rest assured, there is no need for excessive worry when it comes to verifying your credit. Intermittent queries are entirely customary and will not have a negative impact on your credit. You needn't fret over sporadic credit inquiries, but an abundance of them could pose certain difficulties. These could stem from the act of submitting applications for numerous credit lines within a brief timeframe, or from the compulsive solicitation of credit reports.

So, it is evident that multiple variables are taken into consideration when determining your credit score. This information is crucial for comprehending the functioning of credit. Additionally, this data demonstrates the specific aspects that have the greatest impact on your credit score. By initiating this initial action to grasp the intricacies of credit, you are concurrently embarking on a trajectory towards cultivating a more robust credit history, which will inevitably culminate in an elevated credit rating. This will afford you future prospects. Within the following chapter, we will delve into effective methodologies that can be employed to enhance your credit standing.

Your financial resources exert a significant impact on the quality of your lifestyle. As an illustration, it establishes the parameters of your actions and restricts your movements. It is crucial to acquire the skills for effectively managing personal finances in order to achieve both present and future aspirations in life. It is essential to possess knowledge regarding prudent allocation of finances, including discerning expenditure choices, appropriate moments for saving, effective investment strategies, and related considerations. To put it differently, numerous actions that contribute to personal happiness are inherently connected to financial means. Lacking it would render their acquisition impossible. However, it is crucial to acknowledge that the ability to fulfill one's desires through monetary means should not be mistaken for unlimited spending, as excessive expenditures can pave the way for discontentment. To put it differently, should you discover yourself exhausting all your finances and occasionally resorting to borrowing, all in the pursuit of attaining that sense of contentment, it is safe to say that genuine happiness eludes you. Instead, what you experience is a myriad of negative emotions, such as fear, concern, unease, and despair, all stemming from your incapacity to lead the life you desire. Therefore, it can be deduced that your financial satisfaction is heavily contingent upon your competence in efficiently handling and controlling money in accordance with your desires.

Budgeting is an indispensable component within the entire process. Regardless of one's income, the inability to effectively handle finances through prudent budgeting renders one unable to achieve wealth. Regrettably, these abilities are not included in the conventional curriculum of schools. Consequently, a significant number of individuals acquire this knowledge through personal experience when they become indebted or find themselves constrained to a paycheck-to-paycheck existence. With such a lifestyle, your finances are effectively dictating your choices, as you prioritize immediate gratification rather than allocating resources towards essential aspects of your life, ultimately leading to the realization that these crucial priorities have been neglected. In this instance, we perceive savings as the surplus funds that ensue subsequent to the expenditure of our essential financial resources. Nevertheless, it should be noted that the concept of saving extends beyond the mere accumulation of what remains after expenses. Adhering to such a perspective is bound to impede any attempts at saving, as human needs inherently tend to be insatiable.

Effectively managing your finances necessitates assuming responsibility for your financial resources, rather than allowing them to dictate your actions. By adhering to a financial plan, you guarantee a consistent allocation of funds to sufficiently meet your essential needs. Could you kindly provide an explanation of the concept of budgeting?

Budgeting Defined

A more formal way to express the same idea could be: "From a comprehensive perspective, a budget entails the deliberate apportioning of financial resources towards specific objectives." A budget can be defined as a comprehensive strategy outlining projected income and projected expenses for the future. It serves as a valuable and practical framework for acquiring knowledge on effective budgeting and financial planning. An effective budget guarantees timely payment of all your expenses, prepares you for unexpected circumstances, and ultimately enables you to achieve your financial objectives. The aim of budgeting is to ensure that you spend less than what you earn.

It is regrettable that certain individuals tend to perceive budgeting as a means of self-deprivation, thereby conflating it with financial difficulties. In juxtaposition to that notion, budgeting serves as a tool that assists individuals in managing their expenses. I previously alluded to the notion that budgeting entails a conscientious approach to allocating financial resources to various necessities. When considering the broader perspective, adhering to a budget facilitates intelligent financial management. Furthermore, it should be emphasized that while many individuals turn to budgeting in response to financial difficulties, it is intended to be a proactive measure rather than a reactive one.

Have you ever pondered the rationale behind the implementation of budgets among both public and private institutions, notwithstanding their sufficient financial resources? The key aspect at hand is straightforward - in the absence of a budget, there exists no financial plan, thereby leading to a state of financial uncertainty. As previously stated, a budget is a meticulously crafted financial plan. In accordance with the proverbial adage, lacking a plan will result in any path leading to the same outcome.

Budgeting As a Process

As we have observed, budgeting extends beyond the realm of individual financial management—it is an intricate process that necessitates meticulous handling and prudent consideration. In enterprises of considerable size, the budgeting process entails a collaborative effort whereby every department formulates its individual budget prior to a thorough assessment of the relevant and less relevant components. In this scenario, the budgets typically serve as a forecast for the upcoming fiscal year. The operationalization of the budget occurs solely subsequent to its approval.

Not all enterprises necessitate budgeting; there exist certain small-scale businesses that strive to function without a structured budget, although this generally proves to be unfavorable in its consequences. They fail to capitalize on the benefits typically associated with budgeting. A point often overlooked is that, for aspiring entrepreneurs in the start-up phase, the budget functions as a strategic guide for the business. Through the establishment of a consistent budget, one can ascertain the performance of the business. They can additionally function as a means to attract investors, as they enable the presentation of the business's historical performance.

The identity of the user holds no significance; currency retains its intrinsic value. If you have acquired it, it is necessary to allocate sufficient funds for it. To provide clarity on the significance of acquiring proficient money management skills, let us briefly examine several advantages of strategic financial budgeting.

Through acquiring the knowledge of financial management, specifically budgeting, you will:

Alleviate financial pressure and help you remain punctual with your financial obligations.

Allocate your funds to the locations of utmost significance.

Establish attainable objectives and derive satisfaction from the positive aspects of existence.

Achieve success in your endeavor to break free from the cycle of relying solely on one's salary for sustenance.

Discover a heightened level of ease in achieving debt freedom. It also helps you determine if you really can take debt and how much you need

Discover a more manageable approach to curbing or, at the very least, reducing impulsive expenditures.

Acquire the skill of managing your expenditures within your financial limits. Master the art of maintaining a lifestyle that aligns with your financial resources.

Have the capacity to fulfill your family's financial requirements

Maintain a high level of concentration on your financial objectives.

Be sufficiently equipped to anticipate and accommodate unanticipated expenditures." or "Ensure readiness to mitigate unforeseen expenses.

Achieve the ability to reduce conflicts concerning finances with your romantic partner.

To commence, allow me to provide you with a brief outline of the essential steps involved in creating a budget. Although you likely possess familiarity with the process, it is imperative to acknowledge that achieving the discussed benefits entails considerably more than devising a sound plan.

Now, let us delve into the particulars:

Please be advised: As we commence our endeavor, it is imperative to retain focus and remain steadfast, irrespective of the challenges we may encounter throughout the journey.

Similar to how organizations allocate project-based budgets and smaller budgets for departments, individuals may also find it necessary to formulate various types of budgets. Let us examine these.

www.ingramcontent.com/pod-product-compliance
Lightning Source LLC
Chambersburg PA
CBHW050233120526
44590CB00016B/2065